# The Hauntings

Gail Waldstein

Swan Scythe Press

## ACKNOWLEDGEMENTS

My thanks to the editors who published early versions of these poems in:

*I-70 Review*, summer/fall 2013: "a pathologist's prayer" and "Luxembourg encore"
*Seven Hills Review*, vol. 17, 2012: "a vase of lonely"
*The Poet's Billow Literary Galley*, finalist, winter 2013: "larva"
*The Broad River Review*, vol.45, spring 2013: "stark"
*Pearl*, #35, 2006: "wild wedding"
*The Silver Lode*, Columbine Poets Anthology, 2003: "adobe flesh storm"
*The Comstock Review*, vol.27:1, spring/summer 2013: "hymn" and "cancer's reel"
*Switched on Guttenberg*, issue 19, fall 2013: "hypnagogic love"
*Rock & Sling*, vol.4:1, summer 2007: "water baby"
*Seven Hills Review*, vol.19, 2014: "runnel"
*Encore NFSPS Prize Poems*, 1st Winner's Circle, 2008: "qualify"
*The Examined Life*, vol.1 no.2, fall 2011: "stain"
*Puerto del Sol* Poetry Contest, 1st Prize, 2014, to be published 2015: "embryo pathology"
*So to Speak*, to be published fall 2014: "the k sound"
*Encore NFSPS Prize Poems*, 3rd, WyoPoets, 2008: "fetal pig"
Arapahoe Community College Competition, 2014: "the cliffs"
The William Faulkner-William Wisdom Contest, 1st Prize, 2013: "rapid"
*The Double Dealer*, 2013: "rapid"

I dedicate this chapbook to my children Sarah, Samantha and Saul who have loved and supported me for decades, and to my grandchildren with whom love is physical, palpable and pure. And especially because this new generation still reads poetry: Mack, Jasper, Calli, Benjamin, Oscar and Viviane.



ISBN 978-1-930454-41-5

Swan Scythe Press
1468 Mallard Way
Sunnyvale, CA 94087
www.swanscythe.com

*Editor*: Robert S. Pesich
*Associate Editors*: James DenBoer and Calder Lowe
*Founding Editor*: Sandra McPherson
*Book Design, Production & Cover Design*: Mark Deamer and Laura Galbreath
*Cover Art*: Reven Marie Swanson, "Scribbles", www.revenswanson.com

# The Hauntings

# TABLE OF CONTENTS

*The past does not haunt us. We haunt the past.*

Augusten Burroughs

**a pathologist's prayer**


what I see first is a          child's corpse
naked on a steel gray      morgue table
my work so long
swallowing hard against soured
stomach curds              hiding those tidy
faces    beneath surgical towels
as if their stone-open eyes
didn't speak, as if their mouths
hadn't begged for honey      or Mama
as if those tidal fists            limp and flat
hadn't reached    just yesterday
for hair, an earring

as if they no longer feel
yet what if

and who are we who      scalpel, probe
claw for clues
desecrate bodies
as if naming disease        delivers us

our flesh still warm, we suck air
bite our nails, go home to bed
feast on uranium

but at night
when he's done with me
I wonder if
                        some thing of them hovers

a skull vibrating after a tuning fork's
removed    the umbra of a hand protecting
a lash      cutting her cornea

**a vase of lonely**


my daughter says  *empty*
*vases are sad*        mouths howling
for food or love or      maybe

I make that part up          we walk through
her Paris basement where the
cave wine cellar     homes bottles

shelves of excess     boxed glass
marbles to fix stems
her lover buys her flowers, often

I do too     when I visit
it's Paris vendors adorn
corners   even in pockets

of January freeze  when she calls
homesick          I fly over          retired now
and      she asks so little

works through my visit
I spend days      honing ways
to close in on her

again      like we fell together   weekends
she in Illinois    I, Ohio doctor
she        growing to prime

I, seeping from mine
we climb stairs
pass a forest of vases

she whispers
                *empty, waiting*
and I think—in a flash—when she was

five       drew a nurse
big kindergarten drawing
*what I'll be when I      grow up*

*why nurse?* I asked
*so I can come home    and be*
*with my children*            I saw

how hollowed a cavity
I'd given her
called it childhood, called it love

**helium**


my father's      bedside

breathing stops
starts
he clasps my hand
iron will
bionic grasp
pulls me    to him
to his lips
parched with the labor of   biting air

outside      green palm fronds   slap
pink adobe walls
a small window     curtains rain

balloons suss       *getwell*
bracket us

he's sullen since his stroke
tugs my hand again
like a stutter
in       and in
one last command
                        *stroke me*

I'm fifty now        my own grown woman
reply so slow            first *no*    ever
a voice so young, so high
is it       mine   or
                        balloon air

**larva**


once    there was a girl who loved
pollywogs    little black ones   slimy
green water    beside the creek
dank puddles        creatures soft
and slippery as the inside

of her mouth    her father showed her
made her touch        watch them grow
green splotched skin        then bones
little legs        fins and tails shrank
she stroked them firming

metamorphosis
something in that      rapture
of nature    the stillness and her Dad
not teasing or beating or invading
simply      *see,* he too in awe

when she grew up    she loved biology
became a doctor          learned to try
everything new    with her first
husband        in the end, and there was
one        with each man      she

sampled garlic snails        frog-legs
loved earth-flavors      the slight grit
watery texture    travel and love-making
no longer green      she wonders if change is
still possible   crinkled adult

**stark**


wild white hair      a
horizontal waterfall

her scaffold of bones
sheeted            in a chair

between porch and
flybycars

sun stroked     face   bare
feet purple    beside one crocus

her heart          an
ampersand

**a duet of novices**
>> *first marriage*


opulent lava    onyx beach   Oregon
stones suck our soles in     curl

arches before we swim
water so green

our skin grows eyes
we are lapped and cooled by waves

I braid hair    raven then
as the coastal pebbles you palm

surfaces  supple as fetal
membranes    you caress them

our children          my crumpled face
us         a cooling corpse

close the lids              lave the body
our future no longer distant

we spread a blanket     spread
ourselves            almost pulseless

in pacific deception
as if Lazarus might
                    wash ashore

**wild wedding**
> *second marriage*


the day was flush with rainbows
overripe we were  and common law so long
love withered

hibiscus and papaya were rioting
when finally you said      *Why not?*
you sliced plumeria stems, taped them

silver            I held the bouquet    thick and drunk
on scent and hope       you rented a jeep
drove red clay roads

to Molokai's overlook
the pastor, her daughter climbed with    us
in crimson earth which ate       our footprints

Phallic rock, symbol of
ancient fertility       towered over us
along with rainbows    like anticipation

my white heels ran red
my ivory suit              an extravagant embroidery
my hair, a darkened halo

wet with ocean wash      which
pealed over our silence in the pines
I repeated words, ordinary words    have

repeated them a thousand times
to myself since that day              locked forever
in formation     under double, triple rainbows

like fighter squadrons        above Hawaii
about to release      bombs, or pots of gold   but
the day never moved

only the sky changed
all pictures of us      frozen in that heat
the way you stood, slightly uphill, silver-haired

hand on my shoulder, as though you were taller
as if you blue-suited handsome meant
                                    *until death*


we drove the island          mist sprouting rainbows
stopping for vistas   but even then
it was cooling

the vigor we feigned     approaching
our cheap packed lunch
no champagne because of your          heart

fish, steamed vegetables
the enigma of desire bubbling        away
laying there that night        no lovemaking

when we should have spun beneath shooting stars
lying there, naked as squid
solemn as nuns     bare     beside the body

that once was     wet indigo    tangerine    supple as sap
wed                          in a sapphire paradise
no longer loved

**adobe flesh storm**


gray transparencies of rain
sheet me secure
                a teepee circle

breath escapes     floats skyward
an umbilicus
                attached to    a rose avalanche

lightning glazes     brindled ozone
black and white cows     gnarl wet
gnaw     barley tree trunks

vermilion torrents
webbed with womb scent
torn     from sandstone

spill creek banks
logs sail past our     midnight
raucous once as thunder

we vibrated then          low, concave
a thrum in my thorax     still
our hemisphere     resonates

my heart     bruised in systole
purple     cobalt          black
asks                    why, why I  left you

in the arroyo     in the desert     in the middle     of such a storm

**hymn**



safe after years of
       you    stalking
       in a new hall    outside my door
       you    plead

*can I come in*
       accordion-wind
       dries    my tongue
       pebbled    mute

maybe you aren't at the door
       our marriage wasn't    that
       all this is nothing    but
               mutual hallucination

still    you stand there
       pity    history's rubble
       how does the voice speak    *no*
       knowing this particular    refusal
       may be this body's final
               intimacy

**hypnagogic love**
*for our poodle*


day bracket        she
softened me

between sleep
before sleep
and after

nails on tiles
her breath
          by my ear
you     too     gone

**cancer's reel**


the grand deflation: belly after childbirth
after hysterectomy, radical
loss of sensation, abdominal skin numb

but vibration lingers, tattoo's complete
a black feather under her skirt
the woman will do anything

belly nausea: that hole post-operative period
recalling deep penetration when cancer pushed
in, a pain in the cervix            stay

phantom            as palate ecstasy
fists wild strawberries
in meadow-mind

or holding the baby
a completeness
pressured into my body

hunger resurrects            anew
alienation from physicality
since you left

will I        again
August stars, remote as sinuosity
your quiet quirky smile            shadows

mountains        cold comfort as the surprise
choke on spit            laughing
at the thought    we might

memory slurs, my skin holds your scent
we danced in class, tangoed
                        an empty bell, us

**water baby**



*Ridge Home, Denver, 1969*


her head takes
three beds
body flopped    sideways
tiny toddler's size    only
she's eleven
contractures    secure her
as if she were an
        insect pinned
feeding tube    intermittent nursing
sops drool, soil    and the catheter
of course

skin translucent beyond
porcelain
shadow features: nose, brows, slim smile
almost imagined    the way you think ideas float
beneath her vacant, sunset eyes    roaming walls
pupils rolled so far down
the eyes are only white

her rind of cortex thins
despite shunts, failed shunts, replacement
stents    hovering globe almost collapsed
you stroke her forehead
watch for a reflex any reaction    then
touch your growing belly
        pray

**runnel**


there are loves that slip
into you     second self

burrow below   mind-skin
more intimate than tongues

so sprung they will     never release
but you don't know that     then

you live     hunker through
hoping for grace or mercy

the mist     early one morning
frigids

vivid and common cannot co-exist
you know that       yet, yearning

desire   deep     needful   clings
intestinal parasite

you didn't factor the body's
voracity, the hunger of finger tips   and

lips     the insatiable crave
to smell him on your skin

you     haunted, bereft   remain
infested

**qualify**
  *OED: French, fifteenth century*


1) to invest with

    *I think   I love you*
    spoken softly, a closed chapel triptych
    gilt-edged, guilt-tainted, guileless


2) to impart, to make the thing what it is

  *I love  making love with you*


3) to invest with proper accomplishments

  *I love what I know of you*


4) to make legally capable
  (do not think legal, not yet)

  *I promised I'd never  again  never*  you say
  and yet your presence is so  I enter this freely against
            all reason


5) to make (the self) competent for some thing, capable of holding

  me?
  you nuzzle my left breast, I palm your cheek: safe


6) to establish by evidence

  law, logic   gods to you, a  lawyer, a mathematician
  you have your principles


7) to modify (a statement, opinion) by any reservation; to make less strong

  we're riddled by  fears, failures
  *I love you*  comforts  physicality quells
  doubt  but thinking   shrouds us


8) to moderate, reduce to a more normal condition

  *I adore you*  your morning calls
  my sister phones  *let's see how long this lasts*

mother winks from the grave     *if it's too good to be true*

9) to appear calm, to pacify

*nothing prepared me for this          you confess*
*I tell you things I've never          shared*


10) to bring into proper condition, to control, to regulate

your children are primary
you left two wives     one insane, the next unfaithful

11) to modify the strength or flavor

I've never done the things we do          our scent's everywhere
we clasp     in the parking lot     between restaurant and car
we're in our fifties, sixties     unseemly     we risk arrest
we're hopeless

12) to affect a person injuriously

I'm scared, tremulous     you made up your mind about each wife
unilaterally          irrevocably          left them          no discussion

*No   you say  if I love you   and if I'm behind you*
*I'll never     leave you   I swear*
                              always the  *if*

13) to submit quietly

a week later   *I cannot*
*too close, too fast   I'm too damaged*  you whimper


harrowing          reliquary          medieval barber

**before**


daybreak
steel blue    arches

replace night's black
then a pale blue        rinse

like Nana used on white hair
no magenta    orange     red

just shades of gray soften     as
clouds flock the sky

an angel      full wings, gowned body
forms, floats        I'm a child in a

hammock, lazy Catskill afternoons
watching clouds with Nana

skies of Thumper and Bambi and whales
we slide closer        time ellipsis

all those years of bustle and tension
raising my children alone      working

full time          did I show them sky
teach cloud magic

I brushed teeth, checked homework, took them to violin, dance, soccer
what was wrong with me

now          grandchildren        fresh
heavens              elephants morph to rhinos

hippos to humpbacks    we see manatees
green infusion          innocence and play

and oh   the energy      I almost covet
the angel?

figment of a mind seeking
to crayon last days                      bannered

**stain**


unthinkable          an
autopsy on a child          once     in  my  residency  late        afternoon
my advisor in a chair          I  carved          dissected          sweat  into
the field        strained teen organs                              out   of        cavities
thoracic       abdominal      cranial                         he  complained   of
heat    what was taking me so long        me          pressing   my   eight
month belly against steel table's edge                                        ankles
hippopotamus-thick                         my head        a bog of  hormones
                                        *I'm so tired*                              he said


years later          rain              pummeled the morgue              skylight
my diener and I laughed and    joked that                        hot summer
afternoon        thinking our minds          out of that scene   away
as if we were                    normal women          having tea and talk
the storm grew fierce          baseball-sized       hail          smashed
skylight        we were covered, not hurt exactly                        stalled
two hours        picking glass and frozen slush      out of              hair
clothes, sockets     preparing the body
for the     funeral home
                                        hard life, hard death, hard rain


                                        what I can't revisit are the warm
bodies                    warm babies                    death's              normally
refrigerated hours          the veil of                    space/time/temperature
makes dissection doable          no longer     Ashley or Jason     a
specimen only                    unless they're warm          intestines still
gurgling     air sighs              from collapsed lungs                the lie
you're not inflicting pain              doesn't work          denial    no
longer strong enough          those days        your eyes play tricks


a chest heaves                    scalpel          slices     its     perfect
inverted arc          hand-knowledge   you can do                asleep
above the concave belly          below the ribs              shoulder to
shoulder              the time—once—only once—you saw her heart
          beat                    you were in the chest already
lungs    pale salmon              full of air                you blinked
all still              no          respirations              you waited
watched    looked back at the heart    left of midline  normal pink muscle
                    *of course not*          it hung still        in its


white  transparent  sac, veil pericardium          you examined  vessels
in situ          aorta          vena cavae              pulmonary  arteries

cut them          removed the specimen to       stainless steel surface
where water and metal               set up a current      you thought
later, all rational                    —a galvanic current—you rubbed
your eyes hard       wished you no longer       inhaled           stale
morgue air       wished your eyes closed              unstained as
                        her heart did this little magic act—lub

**yellow spandex bustier**


shows me a shelf cleavage          I'd forgotten
I want this but          it's          *your* color
*daisy-centered, solid gold*
not brunette          not like me, not a chance


smashing as a fresh convertible          you
look-at-me          buttercup shade
twirled beneath a child's chin
yellowing skin          be happy
and you were          we were          tight friends


yellow          the wax crayon-sun          every child draws
above home          even when the door's hanging
like a dead limb          done after divorce


yellow          precise as the stamen
in the calla lily          he presented that first
stunning night of love          whispering
to your body          *I knew you'd be beautiful*


I warbled          caution          like a yellow throat
my own wounds barely          scabbed over
it's yellow the bruise blooms          day five


he stalked, phoned          *I miss the light of you*
*Of course you do*          you should've said
                              wept instead


you move far away as          winter
girlfriends          once spring daffodils          now autumn
aspen          turn apricot          gold          baren
and achromatic          this carapace of seasons
                              without

**vapor**


my poet friend's mind          once elastic

hinged    on excess
her midnight images

                                        elegant


landscapes          jeweled
musical   perfumed          informed whole

stanzas      a meadow after    lightning
singed grasses

she's shadowed now      eyes sallow
                                        elusive


ears        once calibrated
the world's words                she   an

Indonesian puppeteer
master of mystery     synapses firing

sideways currents  intense as
wildfire                before

medical mistakes mounted
like float cartilage

locking    damage
subtle        stubborn        stuck

her life unspools
                                        ellipsis

we lose   everyone
                        eventually

**tidal**


kelp pods    glisten green
an entire ecosystem
continuous as shoreline

runs miles of coast
its vines      vein   tufted sand
a single elongate plant

like a parent    alone   for years
now    solo granny
life brings           long undulations

waves        unrelenting
curl    bloom       break
roll the green     tangles

seaside footprints     fill
like the belly that grew the child
then empty      vanish

my children move    cross oceans
return    with their children
reunions     shore us

still    an ebb of
                longing

**embryo pathology**


two millimeter cuts
through an embryo
the size of a thimble          curled

tight as pubic hair
I          fumble with    Wilson's
freehand technique

unlike      my pathology professor
so much knowledge      indexed      in fingers
focusing a scope          dissecting a tumor

I went with him to parents
who refused          their child's
autopsy          bent low beneath their loss

his face collapsed in empathy
                         *we're surgical pathologists          we do*
                              *meticulous, careful examinations*

respectful, patient          comfort in his tone
every one submitted
he never nicked a neck          kept the skull incision

behind the child's cowlick          sutures hidden
on the          casket pillow
he's at my elbow today          thirty years later

no morning coffee          steady hands
I dial the fine focus of the
dissecting scope          slicing time, distance

first cut lifts a          minute gelatin cup
white      cake batter
on      scalpel blade

two hemispheres belong          where
a single cavity glistens
this lost life          translucent comma

**the k sound**


killer                    keening                    crush
          criminal                    cruel                              crisis

the percussive K
          punctures          hearts


woman with cancer          my girl
                              once pink swaddled

body beveled                    bones fragile     almost
                                        weightless

unbearable     cannot
               cannot speak the word
                              carcinoma

her uterus homes a corrosion
                    cannot conceive

my daughter's belly
               hollowed     as a    dredged chasm

her eggs          cradled now          in  a   frigid   vault
                                        after surgery

she tries     to    speak
her      voice          the      caw      of      a      crow

years later          a new sound     curls               cure
a surrogate               a carrying          kindness

the baby          kicks                    my daughter
          kisses          caresses                    re-kindled

**Luxembourg encore**


the sky's alight with swallows
swift clouds        blue billow
topiaried trees      make all the

difference         two years ago
October     same park
different people, my daughter and I

silent     sky chilled     and inked
her ultrasound             freighted
depilated      stoic nude trees

stone statuary             spewed
frigid    sterile water        shaped
like fronds

only the air        floated
unbreatheable

cancer     a treason of the body
wild terror         our posse

leafed squares     green now
Catherine Medici's plan
levels and fountains       play

grounds     wide fields    grass and
children              my daughter leaves
another ultrasound        do any eggs remain

*ovaries move        after hysterectomy*
*15-25 centimeters*
floating clouds of      possibility

a sib for Oscar        who laughs
babbles      stumbles
a year ago        he funneled

through surrogate's womb
fragile favor

**the cliffs**

*Ocean Beach, CA*


small sculpted island        a stump of rock
juts from the blue      with its vertical
creases      wild white wavecrests
irregular and emphatic as       life

surf rolls to shore
the rookery    littered with
black cormorants
far, far below     a soft stretch of sand
shelters white-breasted gulls
like flowers scattered for
luck or love or make-a-wish

the air is sacred here
young men and old clasp boards
zip wet suits         descend
steep rocks to surf in clots
black-clad    they bounce
wait     watch     wish
the perfect curl

a huge round hole      opens
deep to sea       imploded cliff
reveals the ocean licking      like a pulse
smooth black stones       the cove's base

the subtleties of waves
their complex physics
and origin from the depths
elude me     but the ballet of balance
those black-suited men       arms
spread      as if to fly             that beauty
of surfers         sing      strength and youth
and a kind of buoyant freedom
I no longer own

**Daddy**


maybe it doesn't
matter     what you
did or didn't          do
I remember          or is it
false       a kind of
neurologic scramble

tiles in a game of
scrabble, say     scan the board
weigh       which letters
produce high numbers            you, a
teacher            demanded top scores
from me             hundreds

a measure of something     not
          who I was     not   what I felt
when you felt   me          or
slammed the basement door
black-out         your words then
*be quiet              of course it doesn't
hurt     Daddy would never*

do I recall this        is that
possible          a child's mind is
mauve     secret          an aging one
less so             insecure
what matters now is            what   do I do
with what's left

**rapid**


silk light slants                    over mauve granite
in this   grand expanse of     canyon

stone           groaning        hot
the desert weight              like memories
of that girl       I diagnosed

years ago        taking steps
two-at-a time        from the OR
biopsy in hand      fleshy pink tissue

granular     grey bone flecks
mica in stone
hoping   the bone won't    knick the knife

as I spin the   microtome   wheel
close to her frozen block
cold as this river water              fifty degrees

air arcs to one-twenty         here
Arizona's desert              slices breath      like I slice
eight micra sections

peel tumor off the blade with a
fine, sable brush      lift each piece
delicate as lingerie

in pediatric pathology the tint of tissue
pink or blue        means          everything
her slides          a blue wash

dense populations         explode
                                    osteosarcoma


in the canyon    black *Vishnu shist*
rivulets up    from earthcore    like a
slippery   dark   umbilicus

or the ropes which cord rafts
each night        against   river   waves
days blend   below   bends   and   beveled

ledges      sandstone
*Zoroastrian granite*
*angelbrite shale*           names      sage-scented


her knee pain
danced             her dreams for weeks
stopped soccer practice        two months

then            doctors      x-rays
                        amputation at
                                sixteen, sweetgod

wheel chair        prosthesis         grief


at the tongue of   each   rapid            water    speeds
oarsmen shout     *stay down    hang on*
I kneel    two knees    face the froth

grasp the guy rope          tight
knowing only     hope    and    water
survive


years after surgery
love        runnels her
marriage, a baby

her resurrection        radiance
accompanies them       to clinics    check-ups
all clear                silence after

the canyon wren's        decrescendo
breaks each morning
the baby        two, then three             husband solid

her igneous life              her life of
time            until one day    she
doesn't feel well

five years back then      *is* cured
and all she is   is       a little
short of breath             no pain

like day's   end   on        the river
the way sand gives way                 beneath insteps
forces          labored       breathing

like giving birth                 or coming

her desire        an imperative
and       in fairness       more time with
her daughter

her eyes          glaze dull
at the word               the radiologist
shows her        lungs

not laddered rib-rungs
but          galactic          explosions
white against black      as   she waifs      blue

withdraws        to her      chest      cave
time        dwindles at        warp-speed
her disease          cascades

raw as this river          oarsmen chant
*the river won't hurt you                 rapids spit you out*
*ten seconds, max        even big holes*


her sky           scream-blue


you float        past millennia of     stone
purple   rose   greige
beauty holds danger        oarsmen warn

*it's rocks that drown*   yet you know
no   one   drowns   in   stone
she does

and   on   the   river      the water's
two-stories high              grade ten   rapid
your oarsman is          suddenly          outside

the raft          you yank her    back in
we do not     breathe          water
we've lost that simplicity

the young mother        hungers
for air     for her child's hair
auburn, curling

like currents       when water
furls under, flows upstream        eddies
languid    still       cold as    dry ice


her tumors       grow             drugs futile as
oarsman's strength       in that       whirlpool
                              the mother's breath    a rasp

unfathomable       as       geologic time


our river    time    runs    down             porta-potties full
as lungs
the way we let this canyon       seduce us             thinking

the ride is all       the    water       the    rhythm
the world outside        unchanged
like her life       laying her child             down

that last time
the utter horror        of that
                       long embrace

wheezing        and       fighting    until she comes
to me    one hot August afternoon
twenty-one

closeted in the old basement morgue
head and foot        at bitter ends of the table
chest locked in tumors        hard as

riverwalls       I open        her
so young then             I climb       the steel table
wrestle her stone lungs             up       Stryker saw

her chest        as if
                        to free
                              her heart

tuning fork: two-tined instrument which, when a tine is struck, gives off a musical note (p.1)

contractures: fixed or high resistance to passive stretch of muscles secondary to fibrosis of muscles and joints (p. 13)

diener: person of work in a laboratory; morgue assistant (p.18)

Wilson's freehand technique: method of dissecting an embryo by hand with a scalpel into two millimeter sections, while viewing through a specialized microscope (p. 24)

microtome: instrument for cutting thin slices of tissue for microscopic study (p.29)

micra: plural for micron, one-millionth of a meter (p.29)

Stryker saw: precision saw for surgical procedures whose tip oscillates in a way that vibrations are dramatically reduced (p.32)